# The One Who

BY SIERRA ROMERO

ILLUSTRATED BY TJ WONG

**DORRANCE**
PUBLISHING CO
EST. 1920
PITTSBURGH, PENNSYLVANIA 15238

Dorrance Publishing Co
585 Alpha Drive
Suite 103
Pittsburgh, PA 15238
Visit our website at *www.dorrancebookstore.com*

ISBN: 978-1-6491-3449-3
eISBN: 978-1-6491-3581-0

# The One Who

*To my baby sister Eva: If not for you, I wouldn't be here to tell my story.*

# THE ONE WHO LEFT

every day of my childhood my mother made a point to
remind me that
i was a mistake,
i was not worthy of the air i breathed,
how ugly I was,
how no one could ever love me,
how annoying my voice was,
and how the world would be better off without me.

i tried so hard to prove her wrong,
i tried to find self-worth,
i tried to love myself,
i tried to change my voice and my appearance,
i tried to be something someone would love,
but i failed
-a mother's never wrong

"i don't want to live with her"
i begged and pleaded to anyone who would listen
i wonder what would've been the final straw for them
what would've made them see what a horrible monster she was
every visit with her was as if i was drowning
no air seemed to find its way to my lungs
what would she do to me this time
i still can't believe she charmed everyone like that
she convinced every doctor and police officer and
social worker that she was a safe option
she convinced them that she loved me
in fact, she almost convinced me
until the moment they left me on the front steps and my
small 5-year-old body was thrown back into battle
promising to keep her secrets

sometimes i wished she would've just killed me,
maybe than they would finally listen

i want to forgive you
i want to forgive you with every fiber of my being
but i guess time doesn't heal all wounds
and i guess time never healed you

how come you didn't wanna watch your babies grow up
now you'll never know who we'll turn out to be
what college we go to
who our friends are
what jobs we have
who we fall in love with
what our kids look like

do you even care
you should've been there
you should be here

i forgive you for not loving me the way you should've
it's not your fault
you didn't know how
because no one ever loved you like they should've
and now we are in a never-ending cycle of broken people
breaking everyone around them

science states that every seven years your cells have
been completely replaced
that means in three more years
i'll have eyes that never saw you,
ears that never heard you,
and skin that you've never touched
i will be made new
i will be whole and clean and i never again will be
tainted by your darkness
and most importantly you will not know me
-four years later

why couldn't i be enough to make you stay

.

i read this book called 'Homecoming' when i was little
it was about a mom who abandons her kids in a grocery
store parking lot
and they manage to survive for weeks wandering the
woods and city streets to find their aunt
in search for a better life
a better mom

after i read it, every time i was left in the car i
prayed she wouldn't come back
i prayed i could go in search of a better life
a better mom

i waited and hoped and prayed for the day she'd
abandoned me
and when that day finally came it was met with a
horrible mixture of sorrow and relief

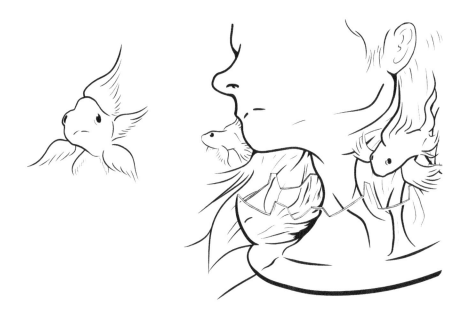

the lies she told convinced even me
her hands hurt less than the words she spoke
i could at least pretend the hits were signs of
affection
because for once she was touching me,
caressing me,
putting an end to my bad behaviors

but why didn't you want me

i ask myself
"when do you stop missing your mom?"
to which i reply
"you never stop, but you gotta remember is, you miss
the idea of what a mom is supposed to be, you don't
miss her."

will i ever be more than a prostitute's daughter
is that all i'm ever going to amount to
her sins forever my burden to carry
can i ever become something greater
-questions that keep me up at night

my bedtime stories weren't those of princes and fairytales
but rather those of abortion, betrayal and rape
i knew i was unwanted before i even entered the world

all i ever wanted was your love
correction: all i ever needed was your love
you were my mommy but i was never your baby

Maybe the issue is me
Maybe the issue has always been me
Maybe i will never be enough for anyone
Maybe if i was cuter or funnier or quieter
Maybe then my mom would've loved me

why did you let them hurt me
why didn't you keep me safe

i still feel like i lost something that was never mine
-mother's love

i wonder if you ever think about me
-your little girl has grown into quite the young lady

i just wanted to make you proud, mommy

my mother put the men in her life before us
so now i put everyone before me
i forget about my own needs and safety
just like my mother forgot about mine

never valued
never loved
always broken

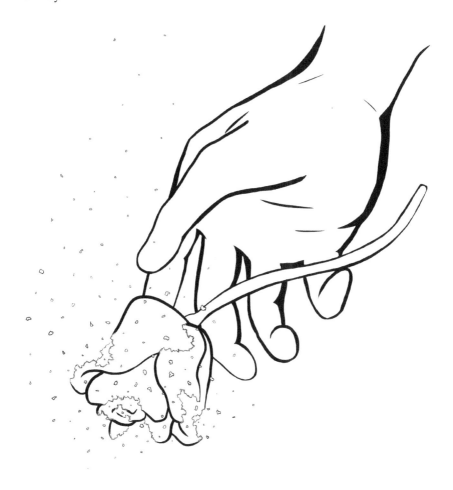

what happens when those you need most threaten your
very existence

i used to wish you were addicted to drugs
or alcohol
or that you were schizophrenic
anything to excuse the mess you made of our lives
something to explain why you didn't want me
something to take the blame

you can't be proud of someone you don't know

i don't know if i'll ever be able to understand the
fact that you're never coming back for me

forever pursuing someone who never pursued me

the one who hurt

maybe we can give this another shot
maybe it will be different
maybe we have learned how to love
maybe we won't break
or maybe we'll crash and burn just like we always do
-maybe

no matter how many times i tried to write myself out of
your story
you always managed to pull me back in
it's as if you know
you'll have my heart for as long as i'll live

i still check on you every once in a while
i secretly hope that you're a mess without me
i hope to see that you haven't moved on
i hope that you think about me every single day knowing
you will never have me back

but i also hope that you have finally learned
that you're getting your shit together
that you're eating right
that you found someone who makes you happy
that you got that car you always dreamed of
And lastly, i hope that when you do think of me you
aren't sad anymore but that you're happy we got to
experience such a love

don't go because i'm not sure if i'm even a person
without you

your biggest fear was getting old
and i'm starting to wonder if it was just getting old
with me that you were so worried about
maybe the cries about your newly found gray hairs or
smile lines were just strange metaphors for all the
reasons you didn't want me anymore
you said being with me was like you found your wife at
only 22
and then you said who'd want to be with their wife when
they're only 22
maybe i reminded you that you had to grow up
that it was time to be an adult
and that job i helped you get and the pressures to move
out of your mom's house must have sealed my fate
-too old for you

i'm not upset that you didn't love me
i'm upset that you let me think that you did

i fell in love with a musician
fingertips for notes and lips for tones
he held in between the chords
but i never knew he played with hearts
tying strings to my hands and feet he made me dance to
the rhythm of his beat

i don't want to be something you can throw away

i keep checking my phone hoping you've texted
proving that you finally thought of me first
that i'm someone you think about
that i'm someone you could be with
that i'm someone you could care about
i hate this feeling
-boys make me feel dumb

when i'm enough for myself maybe i'll be enough for you

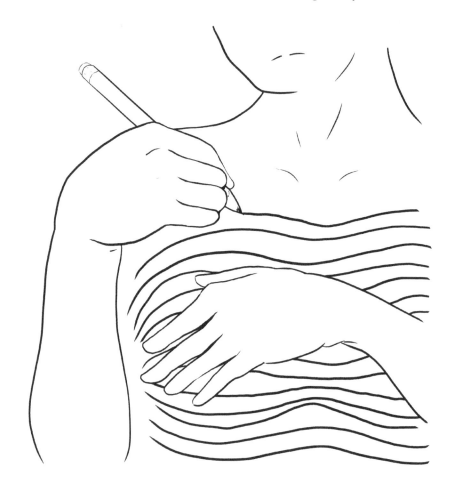

but did you even give me a chance
did you give me a chance to be all you ever wanted
or did you look at me and know it would only last a
night
how charming and convincing you could be
you said everything right
i feel foolish for falling for every word
i should've known someone like you would never take a
chance on someone like me

boys will look at you like you put the stars in the
night sky one day and then like you don't exist the
next

trying to move forward
trying to stop loving you
trying not to tell the new guy about you
trying

you absolutely suck
you're the worst and i hate you
and what i hate most is that
you don't suck and i can't hate you almost at all
you make me fall so in love with you when you're sweet
And i hate that you're not the worst
i really wish you were
so that i didn't love you so damn much
and so i didn't want you back so damn hard

i hate sunflowers because you told me that i reminded
you of them because they were tall and blonde
you also told me that yellow was the color of new
beginnings
so every time you hit me you'd bring me sunflowers to
start over again
and i'd always forgive you

you've tainted such a gorgeous flower the way you
tainted my heart

everyone who loved you said they understand how i feel
but i don't think anyone could ever
they didn't fall asleep every night in your arms
they didn't wake up to your sweet kisses in the morning
they didn't lose you like i lost you
i don't know if i'll ever breathe again
-one month after the accident

how is it that you get to walk through me like a
revolving door
how is it that i'm always here for you no matter how
many times you walk away

i tell myself
"i have to go
i can't stay
i don't want you anymore"
but then you walk up with your sparkling green eyes and
i swear i see my future in them
i want to be strong
i want to say goodbye
i know in my heart, you're not the one for me
but then you walk up and smile at me and i swear i'm
the only person in the world
i know you're only here for a moment
and then you'll be gone
and i'll count the days till you come back
i pray and i pray this time you won't
but then you walk up and say "i'm sorry"
and you swear this time will be different
and i forget every lie you ever told
just like that you're back
just for a moment

no guy will ever compare to you
no matter how hard i try
they all fall in comparison to your charming smile
your kind green eyes
your strong arms that held me tight
i felt so safe with you
now i'm in a constant danger
i need you
i need you
i need you

i think part of me stopped breathing when you left

today i told our love story and i didn't cry
i didn't want you back
i didn't even think of going back
-growth

i still miss you
i search for ways to try and start again
even after knowing what you've done
knowing how you hurt me
i can't help it
i miss you
i miss laughing with you
i miss our wine nights
i miss our star gazing
i miss our long rides
you made my life an adventure
i want that back
- *i need you back*

i find myself thinking about you, even in the middle of
the day surrounded by people, wondering how i'll ever
fill this hole that you left

i had a dream where you asked me to come back
and for the first time my unconscious mind said no
- *you no longer get to rent out my head space*

i keep saying how i've moved on but here i find myself
looking at your Instagram at 2:27 A.M.
i really like that new blue jacket
you've always looked good in blue
can you hold me one more time

the intense fear of being alone has caused me to be
with someone not good for me

i don't know how to love myself but i know how i love
every inch of you
your long eyelashes
your perfect smile
your gravelly voice
the way you pull me close when we're sleeping
the recording me snoring
the proudly claiming me

it's funny because as i was trying to think of all the
reasons i love you i could only think of why i hate you
you're pompous and rude and inconsiderate and a drunk
and selfish and you eat so loudly
and how could i forget
your lack of commitment and how you chew with your
mouth open and how you would always bite me even though
i said i hated it and shove your unwanted tongue down
my throat or the way you acted as if the world owed you
something or the way you'd make fun of my religion or
your inability to compromise or when you'd gaslight me
and make me believe i was the crazy one
or how'd you always make me apologize for your mistakes
look how i came up with so many more reasons why you
suck

- *goodbye for good*

i keep giving you a hundred chances hoping you'll quit
but maybe it's me who should quit
quit you
-how to date an alcoholic

"happy belated Thanksgiving," you text
and i find it funny that you're late with that text
just like you were late with trying to come back
-i've moved on

so sad you finally realized i was what's best for you
after i realized you weren't what's best for me

there will always be a spot for you
waiting for you
to decide you're ready
to come back
and claim what's yours
-i lied in the last poem, i'll never move on

you got to touch me in a way no man has ever touched
before
you were gentle and sweet and caring
you filled me with such a warmth
you held me tight
you kissed my forehead
and then you left
-please come back, i'm getting cold

in reality i broke my own heart
expecting you'd be different
expecting you'd choose me
expecting love
expecting

i only spent 1248 hours with you
it took me 5376 hours with the last one to learn
i'm getting better

i always knew he wasn't right for me
but i tried so damn hard to make myself fit
thought that if i trimmed down who i was
we could be together
-never enough

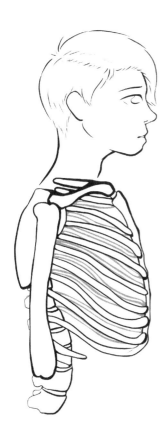
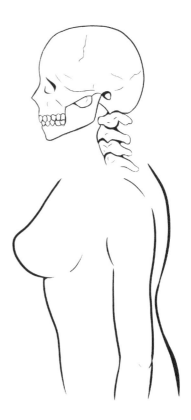

when you didn't fight for me you proved with no words
that i wasn't worth anything to you

i have a type
i look for the emotionally unavailable
can't get enough for their brown eyes and sweet lies

trying to love again but so afraid he's going to be
just like you
-the scars you left

when someone who looked the way you did said they
wanted me i finally felt like i was enough
and then you left and i was reminded that i'd never be
enough
-i find my worth in you

you said you wanted us to be on the same page
but only if it was of your book
i was never allowed to hold the pen

a man cannot be committed to you if he's still
committed to her
-say goodbye to your ex already

i realized i don't miss you anymore
i miss the idea of you
i miss someone holding my hand
and my bag
and my drinks when they were too cold for me
i miss someone giving me the other half of their Kit-
Kats
i miss the idea that i'm worthy of love

my biggest mistake was letting you know you hold my
heart in your hand because that somehow gave you
permission to use it as your stress ball

how did you manage to break me so bad
that even when i'm with a
charming, respectful, intelligent man,
i miss our fights
and the neglect
chasing you
begging you to love me
my tear-stained pillows
waiting for you to treat me how he treats me
-damaged goods

i really believed you'd always be on my side

a letter to the next girl
he's the best kisser
which I'm sure you already know
it's totally adorable when he speaks to you in Spanish
and calls you his gringa
he's gonna give you sunflowers and tell you,
you have his heart
but be careful, he's the best liar
he's gonna sing you songs late at night that reminded
him of you
but they reminded him of me too
he's gonna say "I love you" way too early and you're
gonna say it back because no one has ever held you as
closely has he did
he's gonna go through great lengths to see you
always putting you first
but that doesn't last
he's still texting me and the girl before me and he's
probably texting his next girl too
guard your heart
but take care of him too,
he doesn't understand British accents so you're gonna
have to translate for him
he can't sit through a whole movie unless you're at the
movie theater
he loves his meat cooked all the way through and will
look at your weird when you eat yours rare.
when you bring him his black coffee,
he'll call you his little blondie and tell you how much
he loves your eyes

and if you really do fall for him
remind him that you love him every day because he's
really insecure
he's scared of being alone
so the moment you go away
even if it's for a vacation
he will be with someone else
some other things you should know
you're never going to be right so don't even try
he is the man
he is smarter
stronger
better than you
The sooner you accept that the easier the relationship
don't cry too much when you guys fight, he gets annoyed
but hold him when he cries when Barcelona loses
and don't even get him started on politics
you're white so you're privileged
and don't understand because you're a woman and your
brain can't think as highly as his can
be careful
he can play you better than he can play guitar
i too fell for the innocent, caring, smiley man who
loves Jesus
his heart is in the right place
he will always apologize when he hurts you
he will say he let his feelings get in the way of how
you should be treated
you don't have to forgive him
but you will 5,6,7,8 times
because he will casually remind you how lucky you are
to be in his presence

and that no other man would ever want you
don't be offended when he doesn't claim you in front of
anyone at church
that's where he gets his new girls
but please be sure to drop all your male friends
remember, he's the only male you're allowed to speak to
but that one can be a hard rule so
after he yells at you and tells you you have no
boundaries and all guys have access to you
he will play the song "Jealous Guy" by John Lennon and
that will count as an apology
i'm gonna say it again
you don't have to forgive him
also don't tell him i said this but
even though he's a pastor
i don't think he's close to the Lord at all
i think he's just well educated on the bible
he doesn't really seem to have a good relationship with
Jesus
and you'll notice that soon
just pray for him, please,
the heart on that man is like none other
he just needs the right girl
-from his last girl

i didn't know a heart could break like this
every other heartbreak felt different because someone
chose to leave
but you didn't choose to leave me
life chose to make you leave me
and now i'm all alone
crying myself to sleep for the 7th night in a row
-one week after the accident

# THE ONE WHO BROKE

i've got a whole lot of love to give but all that
spills out of me is brokenness and hurt

every time i think i'm doing really good
i'm reminded of the hurt
and i realize i was just pushing it aside to get to
pretend to be happy
because sometimes pretending to be whole is easier than
actually being whole

i have nothing left

drowning above water
suffocation but still breathing
burning in a snowstorm
don't say it's all in my head
my mind keeps telling me my heart isn't beating
but i can feel it pounding in my ears
PTSD takes control

i don't know who i'd be if i wasn't broken
maybe i should never heal
the idea of being whole is so foreign
and maybe someone as broken as me isn't allowed to be
fixed
i'd rather stay shattered than be rejected from being
whole

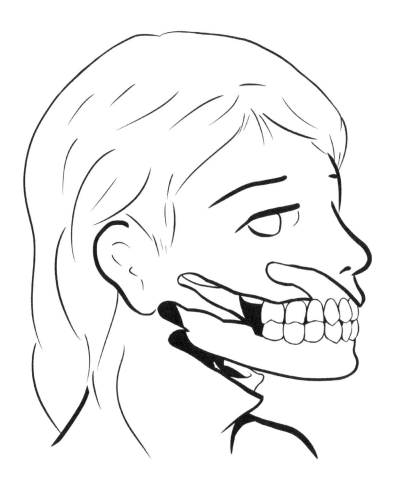

what do you want?
i ask myself
love me raw and naked and bruised and broken
love my cracks and scars and bumps
love my voice and my hands and gnawed at fingernails
love my knobby knees and gangly arms
love me
i answer

maybe i'll never sleep again

i'm not whole until somebody wants me

-you ruin everything around you
too broken
too damaged
i can't be put back together
there's no helping me
i shouldn't be in society

if you grew up in a loveless home you spend the rest of
life trying to find someone to fill the gaping hole
within your soul but each person manages to grab a
shovel and just dig out some more
-forever empty

my parents broke my heart before any man ever got the
chance to
and now i walk around with this big broken mess that no
one can heal

i hate how easy i break down
i hate how quickly i crumble
i hate how i'm a slave to my emotions
i hate how i let people take my power
- I want to be free

my PTSD is from a different kind of war
a war on childhood

but i don't feel so strong
-i'm not a fighter

the people who were supposed to keep me safe didn't
and now i'm afraid no one will

always fighting
always crying
always hurting
never learning

i'm sorry the system failed you
i'm sorry the world couldn't protect you

God, please don't leave me in the depths of darkness

who were you before they broke you

he will leave you because you're fragile
-love notes to myself

when my heart is broken
i don't grieve
i shatter

# THE ONE WHO TOOK

when i decided i wanted to write a poetry book
i freaked out because that meant all this hurt would be
exposed
i knew this section would be the hardest to share
i realized i only had a handful of entries about it
i knew it wasn't enough and it didn't accurately
portray how i felt or my journey
but i think i wasn't even ready to share that part of
me with myself
it's terrifying
i feel as though i have to relive it to write about it
it's too hard sometimes
so
here's the best i got
be gentle with me
i'm fragile

most of these are written as
"things i want to say to my abuser but never could"
i'm apologizing in advance

i think of your touch
and your aggression
and your need to be satisfied by my seven-year-old body
and i'm so afraid that every time the boy who loves
kisses me
i'll think of you
stealing
what was his
what was mine

i feel so disgusting
so dirty and damaged
i can never be cleaned or put back together
all because you felt the need to rip me apart before i
could barely speak

not pure
not innocent
not a virgin
because of what you took from be when i was a baby

sometimes when i close my eyes
i picture you ripping me open
and even after i force my eyes open i still see you
-go away

i can't shower at night
i'm afraid you're going to come back
i'm afraid you'll tear another piece of me away

we've been taught to be on the lookout for the creepy
men hiding behind parked cars on your walk home
use the buddy system
watch your drinks
carry pepper spray
cover up
but can you tell me
how do i protect myself when i'm in the shower and my
uncle joins
how do i protect myself when i'm fast asleep and awoken
by my brother's touch
how do i protect myself when i'm watching tv and my
stepdad can't keep his hands off of me
what will save me then

you took so much from me
you took it all
how do i get to take something from you so you can feel
as empty and broken as i do
-why do you get to be whole if i'm not

i'm so afraid that if i turn out the lights
the men who ripped be apart will come back
but this time
together
and ready to win the war they started with my body

i almost forgot you existed
i became so happy over the year and a half since we
broke up that i forgot about all the pain and the lies
and the fights and the hurt

but today
a women's empowerment Instagram page posted one of your
songs
a women's empowerment page
and i can't help but wonder if they know what you did
if they know about the abuse
if they know that you told me "one day you'll have to
get over the whole rape thing because no guy will wait
forever" because my PTSD got in the way of your
pleasure
if they know that you choked me because i wasn't
listening to you yell at me for an Instagram post you
thought was too racy
if they know that you hid all my clothes you thought
were too revealing
if they know that you deleted all men from my social
media because the only man i was allowed to know was
you
if they know about the time you backhanded me in the
face because i caught you cheating
do they know the real you
i do
and the man i know is the furthest thing from women
empowerment
-fuck you for experiencing happiness; you deserve
nothing

were my size 2t pink flower pants too tight?
or was it my Rugrats t-shirt
what about my 2-year-old body was too scandalous for
you
did i get too drunk on apple juice
did i lead you on during my nap
did you know i couldn't consent because i didn't even
know the word yes yet
or was it just because i was left alone with you
a monster

don't believe him when he says he's only angry because
he cares about you

you don't ever really stop crying

i want to tell them that it gets better
that it gets easier
that you don't cry yourself awake at night after a
while
but it doesn't
and you do.

there's just longer gaps in between the falls

# THE ONE WHO HEALED

The One Who

-to my body
the words i've said about you weren't always kind
the things forced upon you weren't always good
the energy around you was negative for far too long
and for that i'm sorry
i'm sorry for every scar
every bump
every bruise
i have finally learned to love you
slowly
carefully
but finally
thank you for surviving through all the ugly that's
been thrown at you

i don't want to die anymore
i want to live
i want to be alive
i want to live
i don't want to die anymore

dear baby sister
you aren't in this alone
i will fight with you
i will hold your hand
i will save you from falling
i won't leave you behind
you're never on your own

i thought i'd always be the little broken foster kid
with the sad story
i thought i'd always be damaged
i thought i wasn't worthy of love
i thought i would never be enough

until i found God
He lifted me up and told me nothing's too broken for
Him
told me i'm worthy
i'm enough
told me He loved me
and now i feel whole

no more fighting for people's love and affection
no more being scared to come home
no more lies

walking away from toxic people or things doesn't mean
that you quit or you lost
you have every right to leave
do what's best for you
God is calling you to much more than what they can give
you
much more than it can offer

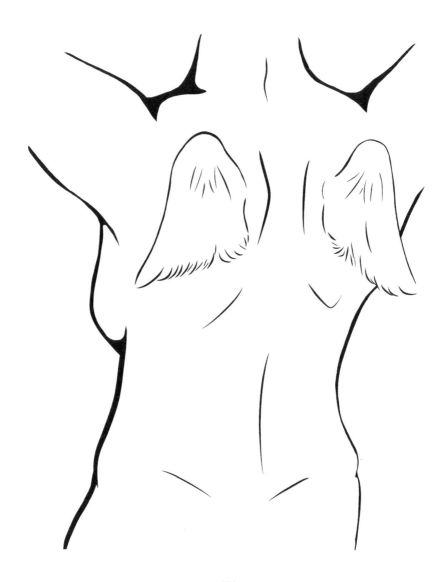

heal
be better
the stress isn't good for your skin

i think this is what a person who is whole feels like

i was so afraid the rape would become a part of my
identity
but God made sure i could find all the beautiful
parts of me

i'm gonna be okay even though you didn't stay

picking myself because no one has ever picked me

for so long i hated you because you got to take so much
from me
i wanted you to suffer so badly
i wanted you dead

but now i forgive you, i don't hate you because you can
not take anything from me without my permission
i'm going to choose to love you, though i will get no
love in return because that's what God does
he loves
and he loved me on the nights i begged for a mother to
hold me but never came
and he loved me after you left me bloody and broken and
hopeless
he loved me even when I deserved not an ounce of love
so i will love you
and pray for your peace
and hope that you do all you've ever dreamed of with
your second chance
-i am free

The One Who

sometimes when i'm lying in bed alone
and all the thoughts and memories come flooding in
and the pain is about to take control
and i whisper to myself how i have nothing left
i swear i can actually feel God reaching into my chest
to calm the panic in my heart

i did it
i graduated college
i beat the odds
i fought every statistic against me
turns out i didn't need her at all

for the first time in my life i have the last name of
someone who loves me
i prayed for this my whole life
i finally have a family

I prayed for you
I prayed for you my whole life
I prayed for a mom and a dad that would love me forever
I prayed for a family every day
I prayed for a place of belonging
I prayed for a place of peace
I prayed for a place of joy
I prayed the last name of someone who loved me
I prayed for you

dear baby sister, pt. 2
i thank God every day for giving me you
you're my best friend
my other half
my person
you saved me
you rescued me
and you continue to rescue me every day
you're my hero and i will never be able to thank you
enough for saving my life

when your family didn't stay for you, that's not God

i'm standing up for the people who had to grow up way
too young

i know we are both better off

learning to love myself
by myself
figuring out how to be alone

i will not let the word "victim" be in my narrative
i will not let anyone make me into something i'm not

boys do not dictate the standards of beauty

you're not coming back

thank you for never loving me
you taught me that the only love i needed was God's

when i was in high school the cable guy was in the
driveway when i got home and asked if my parents were
home
i said "no" and he said "okay, do you know where i can
find the"... whatever he called it.
To which i replied with "no idea, i'm just their foster
kid, i can get their son?"
He said "okay, thank you"
As i went in to get him the cable man said "sweetheart,
you are never just someone's foster kid, you're so much
more than that"

i am whole no matter how many hands have taken pieces
of me

never set aside your comfort for his ego

i'm not disposable

i'll do better than she did
my daughter will never wonder if she's loved or cared
or is enough
she will have the mother i deserved

you were not made to complete me
i complete myself

people kept calling me a fighter
but no one was willing to get in the ring with me
only a few even stood by my corner
cheering
but never helping me win
i wonder how many will take credit when i get my belt

people can only take what you allow them to

i tried so hard to find a reason why
destroying my mind
seeing if we blame someone other than me
was her love only unattainable because it didn't exist
or was I so unlovable
my own mother couldn't love me
should i have begged
was i not cute enough
good enough
smart enough
what child has to plead for an instinctual love

there wasn't enough stitches in the world to repair the
gaping holes within my soul

the best thing my mother ever did for me was giving up
her parental rights
because finally i was free
but free is a funny word to put to it
because every night as i sleep
i am haunted by memories of her
memories of the manipulation
recalling every unwanted touch
remembering how my starvation was only for her
satisfaction

i have to remind myself that it's over
and no one will get to violate me again
because some nights i worry so much i feel my lungs
collapse inside my chest
As i relive every moment

i'm walking through life pretending to be someone who's whole but i'm not there yet i've found God but i'm still learning to trust

piece by piece God is pulling me up from the water
teaching me to breathe again
telling me
that it's enough
i'm enough
i'm worthy of love
and that He loves me
that nothing is too broken for Him to fix
I'm not too broken for Him to fix

## The One Who

my mother's love was something I could never have
but it was something I never needed
because all along He was creating a path
to a love far more than my expectations exceeded
because i have his love
and with his love
i have learned to love myself
and that's all the love i'll ever need

# THE ONE WHO LOVED

you can't get to this part of the book without the
previous chapter
without self-healing there is no love

suddenly all the great things in life are more great
because they are shared with you

you make me feel like I'm a phenomenon

Sierra Romero

i look at you and it's like everything before you
doesn't matter anymore

i love the way your sleepy eyes look when you kiss me
in the morning
i love how if I roll too far away at night you pull me
closer
i love that when we drive there's always one hand on my
leg
i love how no matter how many times a day i ask you "do
you still like me" you never reply bored or annoyed but
with a kiss and a "of course i do, baby"

you felt like the home this little foster kid never got
to have

please don't hurt me like they did

and after all this time you still remember how i take
my coffee

we are probably moving too fast but i've never been
reckless so i'm ready to jump and i don't even care if
you catch me
let's be wild
let's be spontaneous
grab me fast and kiss me slow and never let go

"tell me something no one else knows about you"
you say on our first date.
and i want to tell you everything
the hurt, the loss, the pain because i have a feeling
your touch could heal all the brokenness inside of me
but instead i say "French fries are my all-time
favourite food" because i'm afraid if you see all my
damage you're gonna leave and i don't think my soul could take it

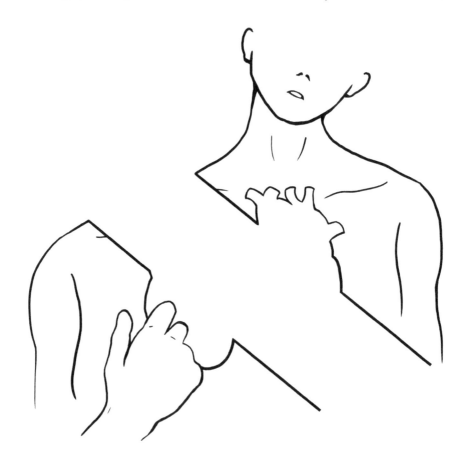

i keep replaying every moment of our meeting in my
head.
the way you looked at me
i want to be looked at like that for the rest of my
life
please tell me again about the dams in China
i could listen to you talk forever
your smile is etched into my mind and i want nothing
more than to see you smile at me again
i don't care who you are or what you come from, i want
to look into your kind eyes every night as i fall
asleep

sitting on this foggy beach and i can't help but think
of you
foggy beaches were kind of our thing
we never meant to come when it was foggy but for some
reason it always was
we'd sit on the rocks and watch the waves come in and
talk about our dreams
it never mattered to me how long we sat in traffic or
how cold and dreary the beach felt
i was with you
and when i was with you nothing could get me down
and now i prefer to go the beach when it's cold
i didn't even realize how much you changed me

that spark of a first kiss
it takes your breath away
i'm ready to fall again
i want to be in your arms for a while
please don't let go
keep looking at me the way you do
this new love is magic

i can't even find the words to express the feeling i
get when you look at me.
all i know is when i'm not with you i'm craving you to
look at me again
my stomach feels like a pancake
no one has ever made me this nervous before
look at me like that forever, please

my head on your chest hearing your heartbeat, our legs
intertwined, breathing synced, your arms wrapped around
my body, your fingers painting pictures on my skin, my
fingers crossed hoping it could be like this for
forever

Sierra Romero

i had this whole world before you
but now i can't imagine any part of my life without
your eyes looking into mine
please don't let my future be without you

i hope I'm so much more than you ever thought I'd be
because you're so much more than i ever thought i get
-thank you for loving me

with one touch you managed to break down all my walls
i've fallen so hard but you managed to catch me
you managed to make me feel whole after a lifetime of
brokenness
you managed to put a joy in my heart
and laughter into my life
you're a dream come true
my sweet angel boy

when you touch me it's like no one has ever touched me
before
just your hand in mine and every scar on my body is
erased
every trace of the ones before you is gone
they mean nothing when i'm in your arms
please hold me forever

did you know that every time you look at me i swear i
can feel my heart catch on fire and just explode into
million little pieces because it's so full of your love
i need you to promise me you'll look at me like that
forever

i managed to fall back in bed with you
and i know you won't stay
and i know this will hurt
but the feel of your skin against mine
and your sweet kisses on my neck somehow make me forget
all that

do i love you or do i love the idea of you?
do i love the way your fingertips trace on my skin or
do i love that i'm being touched at all?
am i capable of a true romance or am i just in need of attention?
-all i know is i need you here with me

we're all just searching for a forever home in a world
of temporary housing and i've found that with you

i took him to the spot you took me in the hopes to
distain one of my favorite places
i thought of you for only a second
new memories are being made now
a new love
a new chapter of a story i get to write

i love you because you always kiss me goodnight
even if we're mad
because you know we can't be mad to kiss
so we have to get unmad so we can sleep
-the little things

you can't leave too
i just don't think my heart can take it

you fill in my gaps
you make me whole

i always wondered if the rape would be what ruined me
for good
if i was now something too broken and too gross to love
but when you lay your hands on me, every defiling touch
just disappears
and i feel clean
my breathing remains steady as i feel your heartbeat
against mine
you somehow have washed away the dirtiest parts of me
by simply loving every inch of me
and i can never thank you enough
for you have set me free

i find you in the darkness

i hope i can be enough

my hiding place, my safe place

i can't imagine ever being loved by another person
you truly are the one meant for me

i love you because you give me the last bite of mashed potatoes
i love you because you always make my bed
i love you because you set little reminders in my phone
telling me that you love me to go off randomly in the
day
i love you because you drop everything and rush right
over when i have a cold
i love you because you never complain when i want to be
held
i love you because you choose me every day
i love you because you remember all the details
i love you because

i used to cry for a love like this
wondering why i wasn't worthy
finally after realizing i needed to heal to be able to
love
you came into my life
healing brought love
love brought healing

CPSIA information can be obtained
at www.ICGtesting.com
Printed in the USA
LVHW081527131222
735135LV00014B/1152

9 781649 134493